THE PROMISE AND PERILS OF EDUCATIONAL COMPARISON

THE LONDON FILE - PAPERS FROM THE
INSTITUTE OF EDUCATION

Titles in the series include:

WHAT WE KNOW ABOUT EFFECTIVE PRIMARY TEACHING	Caroline Gipps
MORE HAS MEANT WOMEN: The feminisation of schooling	Jane Miller
THE ARTS 5-16: Changing the agenda	John White
MUSIC EDUCATION AND THE NATIONAL CURRICULUM	Keith Swanwick
NATIONAL CURRICULUM SCIENCE: So near and yet so far	Arthur Jennings
THE AIMS OF SCHOOL HISTORY: The National Curriculum and beyond	Peter Lee, Denis Shemilt, John Slater, Paddy Walsh and John White
TIME TO CHANGE THE 1981 EDUCATION ACT	Brahm Norwich

For a complete list of the London File Papers please write to
The Tufnell Press,
47 Dalmeny Road,
London,
N7 0DY

THE LONDON FILE
PAPERS FROM THE INSTITUTE OF EDUCATION

THE PROMISE AND PERILS OF EDUCATIONAL COMPARISON

MARTIN McLEAN

INSTITUTE OF EDUCATION
UNIVERSITY OF LONDON

Published by

the Tufnell Press

THE LONDON FILE - PAPERS FROM THE INSTITUTE OF EDUCATION

PUBLISHED
by
the Tufnell Press
47, Dalmeny Road, London, N7 0DY

First published 1992

BRITISH LIBRARY CATALOGUING-IN-PUBLICATION DATA
A catalogue record for this book is available from the British Library

ISBN 1 872767 31 1

Book design by Fiona Barlow, Carter Wong, London
Printed in Great Britain by Da Costa Print, London

CONTENTS

Politicians in this country have drawn attention to foreign educational practice in the last ten years more than at any other time in this century. They have viewed education as a function of global economic competition so that, by implication, internationally inferior industrial performance can be blamed on comparatively poor British education. Political proposals for reform have been backed by reference to supposedly superior educational achievements of other countries.

There is a point to these criticisms. Educational practices abroad have been dismissed too frequently by British educationists as 'backward' or irrelevant. More often they have been ignored. Such responses to the cultures of other countries which are at least as advanced in economic development, as rich in human achievement and as democratic in provision for personal aspirations are quite indefensible. Politicians have sensed this weakeness in the educationists' armour. Ministers have claimed the weapon of educational comparison as their own in the attempt to defeat a recalcitrant educational establishment.

The international comparisons which are given credence by government are flawed. As with comparisons within Britain, of students, teachers, schools, localities and historical epochs, the indicators favoured by ministers do violence to the richness and complexity of differences between schools and other educational institutions in the countries in question. One purpose of this paper is to describe the poverty of such crude comparisons.

Yet those educationists who have constructed strategies derived exclusively from British (and, more often, English) cultural sources are guilty of neglect. The second function of this paper is to explore the ways in which cross-national comparisons can extend the boundaries of educational possibility by helping understanding of what is unique to one culture by contrasting it with others. Comparison is needed which fortifies meaning and which saves indigenous, organic goals from introversion and xenophobia.

The two purposes of this paper are approached by describing the development of comparative education in the context of the British experience. Recent attempts by politicians and researchers to connect comparative educational and economic performance are reviewed. The longest section examines the international studies of the Inspectorate as an example of an 'educational' response. Then the wider possibilities of cross-national educational comparison can be considered.

International educational comparison as enrichment and as impoverishment

Comparison can extend knowledge in a systematic way and so can enlarge understanding. As Emile Durkheim (1938) suggested 'one cannot explain a social fact of any complexity except by following its complete development through all social species'. In the imperfect world of educational policy-making, comparison may also be a judgmental prelude to action which is instant, intuitive, even capricious. Comparative education can be driven by both imperatives since educational inquiry is not a pure branch of disinterested scholarship. It is a search for educational practices that will work in particular contexts. The question is how much inquiry, analysis and information are needed before action can take place.

As a 'scientific' or scholarly activity, comparison of social institutions and behaviours has well established methods. Durkheim, for instance, contrasted the comparisons made within and between societies and historical epochs (ibid., Marsh, 1967). Comparison within one society at one period of time is simpler. Differences between groups of people or types of institutions can be proposed which most observers can accept on trust as part of a shared understanding. This exercise has been incorporated into educational research through techniques of sampling where the intention is to test hypotheses in homogenous populations. Analysis of differences between people and institutions across time and cultural space, on the other hand, is complex and problematic yet is also potentially more illuminating.

What prior assumptions can be made about differences between societies? Some analysts such as Max Weber focused on fundamental divergences between cultures and sought to establish ideal models or cultural types through which to investigate them. Evolutionists such as Karl Marx identified cultural differences as deviations from universal patterns. At most, variations could help to elaborate and strengthen the general rule. Contemporary comparative educationists also divide into universal evolutionists and cultural typologists. So, some have looked for globally valid explanations of educational phenomena. Others have stressed the underlying differences between national educational cultures which no universal law can subsume.

The two camps share some assumptions. Nation states are accepted as units of comparison because state education in most countries has been influenced by national governments, directly or indirectly, and because national educational traditions leave a powerful impression on contemporary practice. Similar economic forces which operate in each country as well as pressures to comply with common international social norms are widely recognized. Comparative education research in most parts of the world, whatever the evolutionist or typological preferences of its practitioners, examines the interaction between global change and national resistance.

Since the mid-19th century, most 'comparison' has been undertaken by servants of government who have pursued in foreign countries educational solutions for the problems of their own systems. They assumed that if country X has solved an educational problem still encountered by country Y then the transfer of an educational practices from country X to country Y would produce similar felicitous results. The 'educational borrowers', however, hurdled technical questions of whether there was an equal causal connection between 'problems' and 'solutions' in both donor and recipient countries.

The discovery of difficulties in cross-national educational borrowing in the 19th century led to greater humility and the acceptance that, at most, international comparison is likely to indicate the complexity of the issues and the lack of instant solutions. These reservations had been noted in 1900 by Sir Michael Sadler who had led the most extensive study of foreign education ever undertaken in Britain (Board of Education/Education Department 1897-1914). The results led him to the conclusion that:

> We cannot wander at pleasure among the educational systems of the world, like a child strolling through a garden, and pick off a flower from one bush and some leaves from another, then expect that if we stick what we have gathered into the soil at home, we have a living plant. A national education system is a living thing. (quoted in Hans, 1958 p.3)

> 'The implication was that educational borrowing should be preceded by thorough and careful study of the contexts—political, economic, cultural, philosophical—of educational practice in different countries, precisely the kind of task set themselves by a generation of comparative educationists in Europe and North America in the first half of the twentieth century.'

Borrowing on an international scale restarted in the optimistic 1960s. International agencies, especially UNESCO from 1963 and OECD from 1974, began to compile international statistics of education based on systematic categories to describe educational provision in different countries. However, acceptable cross-national measures of, for instance, the content of schooling or the effectiveness of teachers have remained as elusive as they were for Matthew Arnold who doubted even the validity of comparisons of pupil participation by which to assess the relative success of different national policies for universal elementary schooling (Arnold, 1964 pp.17-19). Attempts by researchers to establish and test qualitative relationships which would be valid for all countries produced flawed results. For example, the International Project for Educational Achievement (IEA) in the early 1960s, tried to find a link between student attainment and a variety of factors such as type of educational administration, curriculum organization, teacher quality and parental motivation (Husen, 1967). The ambition was great but the achievement was limited. Even the validity of the modest conclusions were doubted by questions of comparability of educational institutions across countries.

This brief account belies any tidy pattern of chronological development of understanding and practice in the field of comparative education. Educational policy makers and educational researchers veered back and forwards from uncritical acceptance of foreign evidence to blinkered xenophobia. The foreign borrowing often came at times of rapid educational change when new groups participated in policy making. In the mid-nineteenth century, educational pilgrimages were made by the new mandarins of state education—Sir James Kay-Shuttleworth and Matthew Arnold from Britain, Victor Cousin from France, Horace Mann from the USA—to gather ammunition to attack the opponents of educational change at home (Noah and Eckstein, 1969 pp.8-82).

For most of the twentieth century, educational policy in the industrial countries of Europe and North America eschewed foreign comparisons. The exception was the brief panic in the USA in 1957-58 about a superior Soviet school which allowed the USSR to put the first man in space which spawned some comparative studies (e.g. Bronfenbrenner, 1970). Not until the 1980s did national government agents in western industrial countries, notably the United States and Britain, again look abroad to support their demands for change in face of opposition from traditional educational establishments. Little was learned over the hundred and fifty years. Borrowing again was crude and partial.

The latest phase of international comparison in Britain confronted conceptions of education, espoused by the educational establishment, which had little place for comparative study. Educational philosophy, psychology and sociology, as they developed from the 1940s, started from universal concepts which might be elaborated by reference to an international literature (though predominantly from the USA) which were applied almost exclusively to British education and society. The absolutes identified in the search for a British educational authenticity included individuality, community, morality, rationality and intelligence, feeling and physical identity. Each aim assumed integrity of outcomes measured against an ideal person, society, knowledge and experience. Any kind of comparison appeared redundant since the only standard was the judgement of practice against the prescribed ideal.

The overriding assumption was that authentic educational processes are organic. Concepts of the 'whole' child suggested that education should be organized to encourage the development of his or her natural growth towards a unity of endogenous meaning and experience. The creation of a community to fulfil the social needs of individuals has been the basic educational aim expressed in many twentieth century philosophies. The unity of morality, thought and knowledge which concerned Confucius and Plato remained the point of departure for many modern educationists.

In each scheme the aims were often so grandiose that they seemed remote from the reality of school practice. Developments in educational inquiry emphasized that processes could vary according to circumstance and the interpretations of individual participants. The outcome was relativism and atomization. In Britain in the 1970s the heuristic search for the aims which actually prevailed in each specific educational location was informed by phenomenological views, by methods of ethnography and classroom observation (for instance, Walker and Adelman, 1975). The case study was elevated as the empirical means to discovery of locationally specific aims. Educational research and theory in Britain moved even further from a broad international overview of educational developments.

The abandonment of overt or uniform definitions of educational authenticity permitted politicians to propose their own educational aims related to occupational opportunity and to uniformity of standards. The concern was not how far students, teachers and schools met ill-defined latent possibilities but how they performed against each other by whatever criteria could be made to apply to them. Comparisons concentrated on the lowest common denominator. What was measurable counted instead of what mattered.

There was another weakness in the dichotomy in educational research between grand theory and micro-studies. Beneath the apparent democratization of theory and practice was often a hidden chauvinism which permitted the survival of very traditional and Anglocentric conceptions. Foreign versions of authenticity were rarely accepted. The moral superiority of 'education' over 'training' was maintained in face of political demands for schools to prepare young people for work despite the existence in other cultures of traditions which united the two, like that in Germany stretching from Immanuel Kant to Georg Kerschensteiner (Kant, 1899, Simons, 1966). The leap that was made in the USA in the nineteenth century from regarding school knowledge as valuable for its own sake to a view that knowledge was valuable primarily for its use—a concept that applied in practice before the philosophical analysis of pragmatists such as John Dewey—was rejected when it began to reach Britain through curriculum projects such as *Man: a course of study* (Jenkins, 1980). Continental European ideas—expressed in the 17th century by John Amos Comenius (1907)—that standardized, uniform curricula could be egalitarian and democratic—were ignored in the commitment to student individualism and an all-powerful role for every teacher. Eastern Confucian ideas that it was the moral quest for learning that mattered and not the content of education (Dore, 1984 pp.180-204) had almost no impact. The internal democratization of aims of education was accompanied by the erection of national tariff walls against educational ideas from other cultures. And the educational autarkists were found at every point of the political and ideological spectrum.

While the politicians had been presented with opportunities to wrest the control of aims from the educationists and to define them in hard terms which included international comparisons, the educationists had failed to embrace a more liberal, empathetic approach to international educational experience. They allowed the politicians to claim this dimension for themselves and to use it in their own ways for their own purposes.

However, the resurgence of comparative approaches to education in the early 1980s was not simply a result of self-immolation by educationists. There had been major changes in the world economy in the 1970s which drove politicians to more international perspectives. There seemed to be a real crisis for British education in the 1970s and 1980s which most participants eventually recognized, and this crisis had global dimensions.

The imperatives of contemporary cross-national educational studies

The emergence of high technology production after the 1974 oil crisis, especially in Japan and Germany, with the consequent development of automated and computerized manufacturing had profound implications for the labour force. The majority of workers had to develop higher levels of cognitive skills in literary, numerical and spatial areas as well as the capacity to operate logically organized sub-systems of production. Average students in schools thus had to achieve higher intellectual levels if they were to be capable of participating effectively in the training schemes which were the sine qua non of employment outside the marginal and depressed segment of the labour market.

Relative economic underperformance in Britain and the USA compared with Japan and Germany appeared to have an educational element. Low standards of educational achievement were held responsible in the USA for economic uncompetitiveness (National Commission on Excellence in Education, 1984). This issue threatened to become even more serious in Britain as the move towards a Single European Market put British workers in direct competition for jobs with continental counterparts. It was necessary to compare educational achievements for the whole population in Britain with those of other countries. These international standards would provide the ultimate measuring rod for British education. The politicians, including Secretaries of State for Education Keith Joseph and Kenneth Baker (DES, 1986, 1987a, 1989a), were quicker to appreciate the situation than many educationists.

The new calculus of educational performance should be treated with some caution. There are more complex issues than have been recognized in the conclusions of politicians and the media. So, for instance, global economic movements have implications for wider aspects of education. Schools may need to be more sensitive to cultural diversity to respond to the migration—both inward and outward—that economic change encourages (see McLean, 1990).

If a purely economic-occupational perspective is taken, there are important subsidiary question about the relative importance of factors besides education in labour productivity. Investment is important as well as labour, while worker effectiveness depends also upon industrial relations, managerial efficiency and working practices in addition to those relating to education. Indeed one of the difficulties in analyzing the educational contribution to labour productivity has been the concentration of most labour market studies on these other issues (for instance, Ryan, 1991). There has been a lack of overall analysis of the labour market and educational provision, which necessarily would involve both labour market specialists and educationists who have operated hitherto in ignorance of each other's field.

More detailed investigation might consider, for instance, the kinds of qualities needed by workers. Proposals about necessary literary and numerical attainments and more general logical, systematic thinking skills were made by the Manpower Services Commission and have been introduced into further education courses (DES/HMI, 1990c). Yet questions have not been answered about the relative importance of convergent intellectual capacities compared with other attributes including, for instance, the ability to work in small cooperative groups, the aptitude to think and act independently or creatively, and traditional qualities such as industriousness, loyalty and commitment. At the time when British and Americans were concerned with the higher average educational attainments of Japanese workers, the Japanese government and large companies were worried mainly about the lack of creative, inventive and original thinking among these workers which they blamed on the educational system (Goodman, 1990).

Japanese fears should not however encourage British complacency. British industry may continue to require a higher level of convergent intellectual skills among the majority while the minority of divergent and creative thinkers the education system encourages may not be exploited properly in the British economy. Despite the economic globalization there may be specific attributes of work in Britain that do not apply elsewhere. These characteristics may change quickly in the future just as they have done in the past. Behind the 'hard' evidence of international educational league tables is a lack of enunciation of clear relationships between education and work as they affect specific national economies. The recommendations of the much maligned Plowden Committee were supported partly by assumptions about changes in the nature of work (DES, 1967). That these predictions turned out to be insufficient is of little comfort when contemporary analyses are no more soundly based.

Three major aspects of comparative educational performance have been identified as important for economic achievement—the intellectual attainments of average students; levels of participation in post-compulsory education; and the effectiveness of schemes of vocational training. Comparative analysis of education in this country in recent years has focused on these three areas. Each kind of comparison draws upon techniques which, even when properly applied, have particular weaknesses which should be considered in greater detail.

Comparative studies of the failings of British education

Student attainment

The starting point of much debate has been the correlation between league tables of student attainment and those of overall economic performance. The origin of these comparisons lay in the ambitious intention, referred to above, of the IEA in the early 1960s to relate student attainment to a number of educational and social variables. The relative performance of 13-14 year olds and, to a lesser extent, of 17-19 year olds in common mathematics tests had the greatest impact, especially those which showed much higher levels of achievement of 13 year olds in Japan and some other industrial countries compared with England or the USA (see Appendix). A repeat of the tests in 1982 showed the differences between countries had changed little while other testing agencies suggested later that some newly industrializing countries such as South Korea, Taiwan and China as well as such eastern European states as Hungary were challenging Britain and the USA (Lapointe, Mead and Philips, 1989, Foxman, 1992). These results were confirmed by smaller scale testing in Britain and Germany (Prais and Wagner, 1985).

These tests fall within the evolutionist approach to comparison. At a very broad level, the correlations between student achievement and economic performance have a powerful impact. Government ministers, who gave much credence to the comparable economic indicators such as economic growth rates or indices of labour productivity, were offered an educational equivalent. Education Secretary

Kenneth Baker used the international league tables to criticize mathematics teaching in England and Wales (DES, 1988). Yet there are difficulties in establishing causal connections which apply to many such universal correlations.

There are the technical difficulties of measuring like against like in cross national studies. For instance, mathematics had been chosen for comparison as a universal and culturally neutral subject—indeed IEA tests of performance in other subjects including science and languages attracted less interest because of national variations of content and conceptions of these subjects (Purves, 1987, Husen, 1987). Yet, the universality of curriculum aims and content in mathematics, on closer examination, turned out to be a chimera. There were questions also about the relative place of mathematics in the curriculum of various countries. How far was it central in some countries—so, for instance, success in other subjects could not offset failure in mathematics in final assessment—but less so in others? What was the importance of different student assessment cultures—between countries where students were accustomed to continuous testing and those where testing was confined to specific stages? How far did different approaches to testing matter—the balance between oral or written, continuous or terminal, multiple choice or open ended? There were also serious doubts about whether sampling of students to test was carried out in the same way in different countries and whether pupils of roughly the same age in different countries had comparable amounts of schooling (Theissen *et al.*, 1983).

These reservations showed that it is very difficult to establish any international gold standard of educational performance when the content of schooling, its structure and forms of assessment vary so much between countries. Successful countries such as Japan or the Netherlands showed as much variation between them in educational practice as existed between each and Britain and the USA. Yet the weaknesses of the exercise, paradoxically, allowed it to be used by politicians and the media. Evidence could be cited to show a problem of low attainments which politicians could feel free to address by their own pet measures. Researchers could not prove the evidence was wrong, simply that the complexities of evaluating it were very great. The reservations did not disprove an international attainment lag among of British students. So politicians could feel safe in their use of simple if unreliable measurements to justify policy.

The irony of later developments in the testing of student attainments was that British researchers, initially hostile to international comparisons, began to take them more seriously and to use them in more legitimate comparative ways while the politicians began to have second thoughts. American commentators (Inkeles, 1979, Noah, 1987) had argued that the IEA results actually indicated that the differences between national mean scores were less significant than the deviations from national mean scores within countries and the variations between these deviations in different countries. Researchers could thus use an international test to explore intra-national differences more fruitfully. Furthermore, the IEA tests showed the British performances in 1964 were, comparatively, little different from those of 1982 which hardly concurred with the received wisdom of politicians on historical trends in British schooling.

The British government withdrew from participation in the IEA project in 1991, a decision which was opposed by educational statisticians on both the 'left' and the 'right'.

This move illuminates the real status of the evidence. The league tables of attainment could provide a fertile ground for further investigation, the results of which cannot be anticipated. They simply alert the politicians to the possibility that British levels of pupil attainment are insufficient by international standards without providing any incontrovertible facts to support such assertions.

International differences in educational provision and participation

While international comparisons of student achievement were used more often by those on the right of the political spectrum, those on the left-centre pointed more to differences of provision and participation of post-16 students (and nursery education) compared with other countries. They drew upon league tables which could be constructed from OECD statistics (see Appendix). Such statistics have been used in public debate to support demands for greater provision of education in Britain.

There are three main hazards in international comparisons of educational provision. The first is that even simple head counts cannot be trusted. The OECD's classification system of levels and types of education is as good as any other though the difficulties of collecting of data means that the international tables are usually several years out of date. Governments manipulate the data collection process suit their own interests. Pressures are brought to modify the classification. National statistics for some countries are not provided. Individual governments issue their own different figures which often differ from those of the OECD. The British government boosted low participation rates in higher education in the mid-1980s by counting nurses in training as higher education students, (DES, 1987b) just as it later claimed nursery education inferior only to France and Belgium by including also day care provision (DES, 1989b). Germany persuaded the OECD to classify apprenticeship training as full-time education in 1990. This last move weakened arguments in Britain that part-time provision should be given particular attention since, prior to the 1990 OECD report, Germany had a total participation rate higher than Japan but a full-time participation rate below that of Britain.

The second difficulty is relationship between participation rates and attainment levels. American full time education for 80 per cent of 18 year olds frequently has been typified as two or three years behind that of Britain in attainment levels—conveniently ignoring the width of the American high school curriculum and its success in developing recreational and social skills. There were fewer doubts about Japanese attainments yet Japan had at least as great a proportion of youth in high schools as the USA. A case could be made that high average attainments of German students were related to the central position of a terminal leaving examination at 16 for the lowest 40 per cent of the attainment group. Yet the status of this examination was also dependent on its use by employers in recruiting apprentices who would receive part-time general education up to the age of 18 as a legal right. Quantitative measures of participation need to be set against qualitative judgements which are much more hazardous.

The third objection highlights the differences between access to courses and their completion. It has been illustrated particularly in higher education where very low British participation, at least before the decision to expand in 1990, was justified by completion rates of almost 90 per cent compared, typically, with around 50 per cent in many other countries. These completion rates could be read several ways, apart from the self congratulation in which government and higher education authorities used to join. British policy limited opportunities by denying many the chance to 'fail' who, in other countries, would then use their upper secondary certificates to embark on other courses. The price of efficiency was a very narrow curriculum in upper secondary education and a lack of connection between general academic and vocational studies compared with other industrial countries.

The crucial statistic which many hope to find in IEA and OECD figures is the comparative educational failure rate. Such an exercise can be undertaken but it would rely on comparison of each country's perception of success and failure and not upon any standard measure. German sources frequently quote the 5 per cent of the total age group who fail to gain a recognized certificate before leaving school at 16—and this magnitude of failure is viewed with alarm (Fuhr, 1989). The French focus on the 20 per cent whose history of grade repeating prevents their completion of full lower secondary education and who either do not enter a vocational craft level course or fail the examination at the end of it (Prost, 1990). Americans are not happy with the 20 per cent who fail to stay to the age of 18 to complete the High School course. Neither are they content with the competence levels that a high school certificate attests. They panic because they no longer have an acceptable measure of educational success. The English and Welsh never have had a widely acceptable standard of success except for five GCSE grade C and above passes which are attained by a minority of the school population. The British are in a quandary about whether a standard is to be kept high by failing large numbers or is to be brought into disrepute by aiming to get more young people to reach it. It is not surprising that politicians who are happy to use international tables of student attainment are uneasy about those relating to participation. Yet very much the same kind of definitional and cultural contextual issues pertain to both sets of exercises.

The most controversial set of comparative educational statistics issued by OECD relate to proportions of public resources and of national wealth devoted to education (see Appendix). British performance in this area has been a little below the mean for the major industrial countries but higher than Germany and the USA and about the same as Japan. Arguments on the one side point to the British government's miserliness and on the other to its cost effectiveness. Neither claim would stand up to closer examination of the impact of cultural and institutional differences, particularly diverging expectations in the various countries about the balance of governmental, employer and parental support for various sectors of education, especially at pre-school, post-compulsory and higher education levels. Nor do these analyses consider educational costs which are the product of different philosophies of teaching—that a teacher-pupil ratio or level of expenditure on teaching equipment or payment of teachers which would be incompatible with effectiveness in the prevalent teaching strategy in one country could be seen as quite adequate when judged against another set of pedagogical assumptions.

These criticisms of international educational statistics do not reject the whole exercise. It is the use of such crude comparisons which is questionable. Quantitative measures have dangers when applied within one country, district or one educational institution. These dangers are magnified at international level. International statistics simply provide hypotheses for testing. They are the starting point for deeper analysis of qualitative differences between education systems. Yet such cultural comparisons have been rare in public debates in Britain.

Comparisons of vocational education structures and provision

Country by country comparisons which are designed to identify differences in broad educational structures which then can be related to processes and outcomes have clear advantages. In the 1980s such studies in Britain focused on foreign vocational training systems. Schools and higher education received less attention. The initiative was taken by such employment agencies as the Manpower Services Commission and the Department of Employment. The resultant messages only slowly filtered through to the Department of Education and Science (Keep, 1991). Indeed the MSC and National Economic Development Office carried out a comparison of vocational education and training in Germany, the USA and Japan as early as 1984 (NEDO/MSC, 1984).

The analysis of national structures of provision of training were taken further by detailed studies of training for particular industries of the National Institute for Economic and Social Research. These showed much more systematic approaches and expectations of higher levels of skill among equivalent apprentices in other countries compared with Britain (Prais, 1981, Prais and Wagner, 1988, Prais and Beadle, 1991, Steedman, 1987, Steedman and Wagner, 1989). The studies of Germany, France and the Netherlands exhibited certain features in common. There were combinations of academic/theoretical and practical/vocational study. There were state vocational examinations and qualifications which were the *sine qua non* of employment in a large number of craft occupations. These studies investigated the content and processes of education rather than simply their organizational structures and attainment outcomes. Yet they concentrated on very limited sectors of vocational training so that their implications for wider educational provision were less clear.

Despite the detailed research, it was difficult for commentators to separate the study of structures and processes from their own political preferences especially in view of the great institutional differences between 'successful' countries. France had a vocational education system which was based upon state economic planning and state educational institutions with employers having a subordinate role whereas in Germany employers broadly controlled the content and assessment of courses and insisted on high levels of initial educational achievement indicated by performance in state school examinations.

Advocates of both systems eschewed explanation or broader contextual studies or facts which did not suit their purposes. The supporters of French solutions gave little attention to the increasing unpopularity of craft type courses at upper secondary level among French students and their parents. This unpopularity was not matched in Germany but the fact was ignored that the craft training system existed alongside a highly inefficient university education where students took on average seven years to complete a degree and unemployment among university graduates was higher than for school leavers. Indeed, the major development in German craft level training in the 1980s was the increasing numbers of 19-20 year old students with the qualifications which gave entitlement to university entry who opted for craft apprenticeship training.

One curious element of the use of comparative examples of training in Britain was the relative neglect of Japan which had by far the most successful economy. There were studies (Prais, 1986, Dore and Sako, 1989) but these had less impact on public debate. Japan's route to training was full-time education for almost all 16-18 year olds followed by training which was almost entirely within companies after employment. The 25 per cent who enrolled in full-time technical schools after 16 largely entered small companies. The giant corporations wanted well educated 18 or 22 year olds whom they would train themselves. British policy makers may have preferred German and French practices than to follow a system which would entail the politically unacceptable policy of providing high standard general education for almost all 16-18 year olds.

The studies of comparative educational attainment and provision were produced by international organizations and by independent researchers. They had the strength that the crude correlations produced by the early investigations could be refined by the continuing research process. They had the weakness that they dealt either with overall organizational structures or with limited sectors of training.

They rarely investigated what happened in classrooms—a valid criticism of a much wider range of comparative work. Like the studies of student attainment and the manipulation of national statistics of provision, the investigations of vocational training at best described the differences between education in various countries. They did not explain in any depth why these differences existed. They offered little guidance on the possibilities of adopting particular foreign practices. At worst they provided ammunition to policy makers who were committed to specific solutions.

The 'educational response': HMI reports on their foreign excursions

The studies of foreign education of the Inspectorate from 1986 are a fascinating contribution to the debate on comparative educational performance. The scale of the operation was unmatched in the DES and its predecessors since Sadler's volumes were completed in 1914. The HMI could be expected to reflect a more 'educational' view than those responsible for the comparative studies described earlier. The methods were different. The inspectors explored classroom issues through direct observation which other analyses had rarely touched. They looked at processes within schools and in higher education in contrast to the emphasis on training in other studies.

The most intriguing aspect this initiative is the possible conflict between an 'educational' and 'political' view of the relevance of foreign educational practice. It is also one that is hidden and on which I have no information apart from the HMI reports and the public statements of ministers. Secretary of State Keith Joseph seems to have been instrumental in bringing foreign education onto the DES agenda. Yet his successors who were most insistent in calling upon foreign examples to support arguments and policy proposals, notably Kenneth Baker and Kenneth Clarke, were also those who adopted the most confrontational stance in relation to professional educationists and who used comparative evidence as a stick to beat the educational establishment. Baker's speech of January 1987 which foreshadowed the 1988 Education Reform Act cited foreign examples to justify a national curriculum and national testing to raise low standards of attainment in England and Wales (DES, 1987a). Each of three major educational statements of Clarke urged the audience or readers to heed well particular foreign lessons (DES, 1991a, 1991b, 1992). In contrast, the more conciliatory John McGregor said little about foreign comparisons except to downplay the international gap in achievements

(DES, 1990). In that context, the strengths of the HMI reports—with the possible exception of that on French primary schools in 1991—was that they took an 'educational' approach to comparative investigation.

The documents themselves have been cogent and informative. Though sober and, at first sight, balanced in tone, they were attractively produced and sold relatively cheaply through the government publications system as well as being publicized by the DES Press Office and sometimes the ministers. They threaten, therefore, to corner the market in analysis of foreign education. Unlike other government and HMI educational reports, the readers may not have the same kind of experience on which to judge the foreign education studies. Whatever the strengths, timeliness and necessity of the exercise, its weaknesses should be criticised. This criticism should be made against the established canons of comparative education analysis.

The first thirteen reports focused on specific aspects of education in particular industrial countries. They were short—in most cases snapshots of limited educational sectors based on brief visits of small teams of inspectors to a few institutions in a limited number of localities. The criteria for selection of countries and sectors within them were the prevalence of some educational practice(s) which had relevance to immediate policy issues in Britain.

The reports can be divided into three categories. Five were concerned mainly with particular phases of compulsory schooling—in Germany, the Netherlands, Denmark, the USA and France (DES/HMI, 1986, 1987, 1989d, 1990a, 1991e). There were also two studies of teacher education (France, the USA) (DES/HMI, 1989a, 1989c); two on vocational education (the USA and Germany) (DES/HMI, 1990b, 1991b); and three on higher education—two on the USA and one on Japan though this last study covered also each of the other areas (DES/HMI, 1989b, 1991a, 1991d). There was also a study of the use of performance indicators in the USA in both schools and higher education (DES/HMI, 1991c). I will focus especially on the reports on schools because they centre on areas not covered in readily available literature on foreign education and because they are based largely on school observation.

The most obvious weakness of the reports on the compulsory phase of schooling came from HMI ways of working. They investigated foreign systems as if they were inspecting English and Welsh schools, even though they admitted that less

Inspector hours went into observation of a foreign country's institutions than was normally allocated to an inspection of one English secondary school (DES/HMI, 1986). They trusted their eyes and their ears in what they regarded as the educational front line. They produced instant accounts which described these reactions.

Methodologically, this approach is weak. It assumes that the HMI would 'know' what was happening in classrooms in other countries equally as well as in those in England and Wales. The exercise was also disingenuous. Members of HMI, from my own acquaintance with the countries, had a much deeper knowledge and understanding of some education systems than others. Some reports do deserve credence. Others are shallow. Many reader might have restricted means to make that distinction.

The result of this kind of inquiry was, on the one hand, a tendency of HMI to criticize foreign schools because they did not conform to English norms and, on the other, to describe areas in which foreign practice may have been superior as exotic phenomena which were noted but not explained or emphasized.

Most frequently, it was the lack of tactile, individual and 'creative' work by children in classrooms that was criticized. In Germany 'teachers said they accepted and encouraged individuality and originality but there was little evidence of either in children's written work seen' and 'to English observers, while the amount and quality of oral work in classes was high, much of the other work seen was unduly theoretical and little concerned with practical application of knowledge and skills' (DES/HMI, 1986). Similar criticisms were made about the range and quality of materials for teaching and learning in schools in the Netherlands (DES/HMI, 1987) and about dull classes dominated by teacher talk in New York (DES/HMI, 1990a). It was as if HMIs could not believe that any teaching and learning could be effective unless students were using their hands for a substantial part of class time. The problem was not teaching in other countries but 'English' conceptions of HMI of what constituted good classroom practice.

If this ethnocentrism was the product of attempts to look critically at foreign education in ways that politicians were disinclined to do, then the effort backfired. The critical guard was dropped in the 1991 report on French primary schools. It was declared that 'French teachers were far more inclined to teach the whole class the same things at the same time. However that is not to say that the teaching was dull or undemanding. On the contrary much of the work in French and mathematics was thoroughly planned, effectively implemented and challenging' (DES/HMI, 1991e). This unmodified enthusiasm, which Education Secretary Clarke used in his attack on English primary school teaching methods (DES, 1991b), also may have weakened the impact of observations in earlier reports.

The HMI had noted examples of much more participatory and pupil centred whole class teaching in other countries—'the general style of teaching in the German classroom emphasizes exposition to and discussion with the whole class, requiring most written work to be done outside the class...The standard of discussion tended to be high and pupils were generally eager to participate. Because there is an argument in class discussions...there is plenty of opportunity for pupil participation' (DES/HMI, 1986). Similar participatory and pupil-centred whole class teaching was described in the 'Kring' classes in the Netherlands, (DES/HMI, 1987) in the participation of pupils in curriculum planning in Denmark (DES/HMI, 1989d) and in the encouragement for students in New York City to develop their arguments in discussion (DES/HMI, 1990a). Yet the cool overall responses to whole class teaching in these countries and a haste in criticizing when they did not meet English norms weakened the power of the positive observations about the potential of liberal whole class teaching.

In failing to explain or develop the accounts of the very positive aspects of foreign practice, the HMI missed the opportunity to make more powerful contributions to English debate. For instance on Germany the 'differentiated system of education and training ... appears more successful than we are in retaining a large proportion of pupils in general education and training until 17 or 18 years of age; in providing attainable goals for them to work towards; and in not hiving off different groups of pupils in ways that can cut them off from mainstream education' (DES/HMI, 1986) and 'the system of assessment ... works because everybody seems determined that it should' (ibid) or on New York schools 'the belief...that "anybody can make it" comes through significantly in the expectations many teachers held for all their students' (DES/HMI, 1990a). Yet the HMIs did not emphasize, elaborate or contextualize. The inattentive reader could be deceived into believing that differentiated school systems may work better or it is just a matter of bringing teachers into line rather than deep seated cultural differences.

Anglocentrism trivialized in other ways, notably in the Dutch and Danish reports. The declared purpose of studying these systems was that they combined nationally prescribed curricula with considerable parent, student and participation at school level. Both reports were short and somewhat superficial. The facts of parental involvement in decision making were noted but there was little comment or analysis. The Danish report particularly was unenthusiastic. Neither the Dutch nor Danish reports displayed the depth of understanding of the educational culture which the first German report had achieved—a more serious omission in view of the lack of secondary material on education in both countries in English. But if somewhat sour bewilderment at alien cultures led to lack of a real insight into these different cultures, and especially on their historical bases, they also lost an opportunity to highlight the sources and operation of parental involvement in both countries, which, in contrast to the English scheme of the 1988 Act, was based on strong and enduring attachments to local communities rather to notions of parents as individualist consumers.

The HMIs may have been constrained by their overall remit, by their relationships with their hosts and by the differing origins and purposes of each study visit. Yet the reports themselves, intentionally or otherwise, provide a cumulative analysis of foreign education designed to show the implications for practice in England and Wales which is offered for public consumption. They are comparative studies and should be treated as such. In that case, the following questions should be raised:

i. How should case studies be chosen ? How far should comparison focus on countries with similar problems or 'superior' solutions?
ii. How far should observers' perceptions be confronted with those of participants?
iii. How can comparative cases develop a cumulative understanding in a systematic way by cross-referencing between the studies?
iv. How do contemporary investigations themselves compare with earlier studies and what conclusions can drawn from changes over time?
v. How far should observations of current educational practice be illuminated by the study of the broader cultural context.

The choice of cases for the potential lessons they could provide produced some curious outcomes. There were three reports on higher education—two on the USA and one on Japan—but none on the EC countries whose systems have already begun to be integrated with that of Britain and comparison of which would seem to be a practical necessity of higher education planners and policy makers. School-based teacher education was examined in New Jersey and France but not in

Germany where it had been established for much longer than either of the other cases. Curriculum and assessment of secondary school pupils were examined in detail in the selective school system of Germany but not in 'successful' countries with comprehensive schooling such as Japan. Primary school teaching methods were reported on in France but not in Germany where the general view is that high standards of pupil attainment are combined, at least in some areas, with more child-centred methods.

Comparative cases, particularly in western Europe, which could have started from similarity of problems with Britain were not investigated. Spanish policy changes in the 1980s have been designed to take central action to counter teacher tendencies to undervalue student performance and capacity (McNair, 1984). Dutch education takes place in a context of long standing and acute divisions between social classes as well as on religious grounds on which, for instance, the examiners of the OECD (1991) commented. Yet this dimension did not appear in the HMI report on Dutch schools.

The two attempts to study systems with similar problems were more soundly based. The New York City schools report did investigate the impact of the hotly debated decentralization of educational control after 1969 and its impact on a city with acute social and educational problems. Potentially this could have provided a more sophisticated comparison either with the dissolution of the ILEA or, more widely, with the tension between a national curriculum and assessment and local management of schools in England and Wales in the context of a city system with which there was widespread dissatisfaction. The HMI had to admit defeat in reaching conclusions in the light of the complexity of schooling and social conditions in New York (DES/ HMI, 1990a).

The report on the use of performance indicators in the USA started from the common problems of great variations in quality and achievement in both countries before reporting on sophisticated American use of indicators (DES/HMI, 1991c) in line with suggestions made by British researchers (Nuttall *et al.*, 1989, Mortimore *et al.* 1988). Again there were difficulties in encompassing the great variety of American education and of putting American predilection for measurement in a cultural and historical context.

The choice of cases is crucial for rigorous comparative study. The apparent idiosyncrasy of the HMI selections may have been the product of circumstances which constrained where they could go and what they could look at. The lack of consistent principles in choosing examples undermines the value of the HMI series as a whole. The HMI did make more reasonable choices than many so-called international studies of education whose coverage reflects the invitations to foreign travel received by the contributors. Proper comparison starts with prior and systematic identification of the most relevant cases. One of the dangers of the HMI series is that it gives the impression that the collection of objects of study was the most appropriate.

The failure of most reports to confront HMI observations with the views of the hosts is a more puzzling weakness. As much, if not more, can be learned about education systems by talking to participants outside classrooms as within them—especially in strange settings. OECD examiners have produced much more insightful views of national systems through such methods (for instance OECD, 1991) This does not seen to have been done at least until the report on Japan where indigenous heart searching was paraded for outside comment (DES/ HMI, 1991d p.1,6,24-25,28). So, for instance, it was noted that there was a lack of real effective means of involving parents and communities in schooling in New York (DES/HMI, 1990a). The great traditional strength of American education has been parental and community support and the great problem of the last twenty years has been its decline in certain inner city areas. Any urban American educationist would have enlightened the HMI. Yet the Inspectors, taking on their missionary roles, had the temerity to suggest that these problems might be solved by following the terms of the 1988 Education Reform Act (ibid).

Asking for local assessment of problems could have provided a better perspective on the reports on German and French schools. In both countries—as in Japan where the HMIs did note the phenomenon—(DES/HMI, 1991d) there has been considerable debate about whether the standardized, external and demanding school curriculum can continue to be applied in the face on growing student alienation and repudiation (Bourdieu and Gros, 1989). Yet this debate finds no record in the HMI reports. In France—in contrast to Germany—this alienation is also linked to substantial failure rates in secondary schooling which are seen to have their origin in hot-house primary teaching as well as in broader cultural-educational values. Of course, English observers may not take these complaints seriously given problems of student alienation and failure in Britain. It does raise questions about whether solutions should be borrowed in England which are already subject to doubt on their home ground.

There is the further issue of how to evaluate the particular foreign experience noted in one report against the overall international educational scene. Studies of student attainment reported in international league tables or bare international comparisons of educational provision of the type provided by OECD have justly been criticized because they are so general and so divorced from contexts as to defy proper analysis. The HMI reports went to the other extreme. They were so bounded by the limits of experience in a few classrooms in one country that the general significance of the conclusions is difficult to assess. The reports contain almost no cross-reference between each other. There is no way of assessing the relevance of the French, German, Dutch, Danish or Dutch reports against each other because the inspectorate provided no means of doing so.

There are similar questions about comparison over time. There was little means of judging whether the practices reported upon in other countries were long established or possibly ephemeral responses to recent developments. This question could have been approached—even if over a large time gap—by reference to previous government work in Britain. It could have helped to counter impressions that the identified strengths of foreign education were the product of decline in English education in recent years. For instance, a government report of 1911 had suggested that French schools 'were much better for training boys of average or mediocre ability' and that whole class teaching of mathematics was superior to the endless working of examples that characterised English schools (Brereton, 1911) except that the English examples referred to were grammar and Public schools. Indeed Sadler had been so depressed by the perceived inferiority of English grammar and Public schools compared with those of Germany that he sought consolation that the ill-educated English would catch up in 'the great and searching examination of actual life' (Sadler 1898). Such backward glances would have helped to put contemporary HMI observations into perspective.

The final criticism of the HMI reports returns to the way of operating, especially the inductive, experiential local approach to gathering information and then framing the broad principles. Differing practices between countries are founded often upon major cultural, historical or institutional differences. In some reports, the HMI made such contextual differences clear as in the case of the German 'dual system' of vocational education which not only was based on historical tradition but also worked because employers had not forsaken their traditional training function (DES/HMI, 1991b). HMIs were aware of the dangers of transplants as they indicated in a paraphrase of Sadler's horticultural analogy in their first report

(DES/HMI, 1986) but they made little attempt in most other reports to sketch the differences in the ecology of national education systems.

HMIs presumably would resist becoming 'academics' who offer no certainties but only more sophisticated explanations for the impossibility of action. Yet, by publishing their reports, the HMI were contributing to an overall debate with a very much wider range of participants who had a right to a deeper analysis. Furthermore, they were better placed than any other group to represent an 'educational view' to counter the exclusive claim of politicians and economists to comparative evidence. Their failure to take comparison seriously at the same time as maintaining their educational values in fact puts education in greater danger from crude comparisons made by non-educationists.

How should comparison be carried out?

The practical purpose of educational comparison is to help educational borrowing by providing a fuller analysis of the institutions upon which the borrowers have designs. It may be also to warn that such borrowing is unlikely to be effective. Foreign practice needs to be examined in the context of the overall educational culture in which it has developed. The study of contexts is a more general, hazardous, partial and theoretical exercise which has not been to the taste of governmental advocates of foreign educational practices.

There have been debates among comparative educationists about how contexts should be studied. On the one hand, there is a need to establish broad distinctions between national education systems so that their differences can be understood in a systematic way (Archer, 1979, Beattie, 1985, Broadfoot and Osborn, 1992, Green, 1990, Holmes, 1981, Neave, 1988). On the other hand, there is a need to illuminate the uniqueness of each educational culture whether in multi-country surveys (King, 1973, Mallinson, 1975) or in individual country studies (Grant, 1979, Halls, 1976, Hearnden, 1976, McNair, 1984). The latter would seem to complement the former though proponents of the uniqueness of each education system are sometimes sceptical of cross-national schema.

The three contextual lines of analysis offered below reflect one style of examination and interpretation within the cross-national typological approach. There are, of course, other schemes. The point is that this kind of analysis is of a recognizable type which is necessary whatever its particular form and whatever the criticisms of the specific analysis.

The questions which inspire 'educational borrowers' provide the starting point. These may be summarized as they have emerged from the various studies of foreign education in Britain since the mid-1980s.

1. Why have schools and teachers in other countries been able to focus on the minimum achievements of average and below average pupils? Why are participation rates in post-16 education higher in most other countries?

2. Why are standardized national or regional school programmes accepted with little debate in other states—especially in Europe? Why has abstract, theoretical whole class teaching survived in the democratized schools of other countries?

3. Why do parents have powerful rights of participation in schools in some countries? Why are teachers trusted to assess students? Why do employers accept the school assessments of students more readily in some other countries than in Britain?

4. Why do parents appear to drive their children to achieve more highly in a range of countries including France, Germany and Japan than in Britain?

The comparative approach assumes that there is unlikely to be one universal hypothetical explanation, which is immediately obvious. It is more fruitful to construct typologies which will help to clarify and to investigate differences between countries. Since collective educational behaviours are likely to reflect long established values of the society and its education system, typologies of educational beliefs and values may be valuable.

The first question about expectations of pupil progress and about participation rates in post-compulsory education may be related to wider *values of social opportunity*. One typology drew distinctions between American folk norms of contest mobility (allowing as many people as possible to participate for as long as possible in the selection race and to reward effort rather than inherent ability) and European, especially English, sponsored mobility norms revealing a belief that a natural elite with inherent abilities could be identified and selected at an early age (Turner, 1971). This scheme was useful in investigating the differences between

American High Schools and the English and Welsh tripartite system in the 1950s. It was useful also in investigating the persistence of sponsorship norms in England after the introduction of comprehensive schooling. Indeed, both the HMI report on New York City and the reciprocal American report on English urban schools (Maeroff, 1991) stressed the importance of values affecting behaviours of teachers which reflect a persistence of these two norms in their respective countries.

This model does not explain differences between Britain (or England and Wales) and other countries of Europe or Japan. An alternative typology distinguishes between collectivist norms which stress the contribution that citizens can make to the common national good and individualist values springing from the social structures of traditionally stratified societies (Hopper, 1971). Collectivism is more entrenched in states affected by the values of the 1789 French Revolution which largely passed by the British Isles. So the commitment of teachers in Germany and France, noted by the HMIs, to raising the standards of achievement of average pupils may be investigated in the persistence of historic collectivist social values about the rights of citizens. The differences between European countries sharing a Jacobin egalitarian tradition are also important as is the case of Japan where social norms emphasising effort rather than ability differences between individuals may derive from Eastern morality rather than American egalitarianism (White, 1987).

These types do not help instant educational borrowing. They assume that educational differences are founded on very long standing values which can be changed with difficulty. Of course they are hypothetical and actual investigations in specific context may reveal more complex alignments. Even such inquiries are not likely to uncover any instant solutions. Success depends on changing values among large numbers of people. Awareness of different values in other countries may give a spur to tackling such tasks.

Values related to the *content of schooling and styles of teaching* fall more completely into educational rather than political arenas of debate. Within Europe, clashes between a rationalist-standardized epistemology, most powerfully entrenched in France but also influential in other parts of the continent, and a humanist-individualist tradition in England are well-known, as are the differences between European respect for the integrity of knowledge boundaries and North American pragmatism (Lauwerys, 1965, Holmes and McLean, 1989, McLean, 1990). These dominant epistemologies are challenged by submerged or subversive views appropriate, as Jean-Jacques Rousseau suggested, to 'man in nature' as opposed to 'man as citizen'(Rousseau, 1911).

Such national epistemological divergences can operate at very different levels. They may lead to a differing status for school subjects so that French upper secondary education gives such a preeminent standing to the mathematics-physical science branch that it influences the whole of lower secondary schooling in a way unknown in Britain. The regard for theoretical, logical, abstract, deductive thinking in the rationalist tradition may be expressed in the content of almost all subjects and also in their didactics. So the whole class teaching method is ultimately related to the dominant epistemology. The empirical, heuristic, sensory, moral and individualist approach which the HMIs found lacking in so much teaching elsewhere is a English cultural phenomenon. Educationists elsewhere may admire its strengths while disapproving of its lack of economy, but equally would find difficulty in detaching it from its wider culture.

The alien epistemology in other parts of Europe may have tempted the HMIs and politicians to develop greater affection for the apparently decaying educational system of the USA as the source of models to copy. Yet American values can be equally foreign, if in different ways. American pragmatic views of the content of education and its teaching, on the one hand, can liken schooling to factory assembly line production and, on the other, to the ideal co-operative and egalitarian rural community (Kleibard, 1987, Lauglo, 1983).

The use of comparative evidence in the debate in England and Wales about national curriculum and 'whole class' teaching has been weak because both politicians and educationists have failed to locate the issues within such frameworks. The identification of deep-seated cultural origins of national differences does not help borrowing but it should illuminate understanding of possibilities within Britain.

Cultural differences of values about *educational power and participation* are known through political attempts to distinguish between a 'free market' philosophy in Britain from continental corporatism—though there would be questions about whether the British type of political/administrative values affecting behaviour is best described as a free market type. Yet this distinction can operate at the level of how parents, teachers and employers regard themselves in relation to public or state educational institutions (McLean, 1988). The democratic formulation that all belongs to the state but the state belongs to all has few British reflections, except in some, now subterranean, beliefs of the political left.

Yet these values can underpin the 'loyalty' that teachers have to a national curriculum and the 'trust' that the society has in the judgements of one group, the teachers both individually and collectively, in assessing children—a loyalty and trust missing in the confrontational, yet privatist separation of state and society in Britain. Teachers in other European countries are often civil servants which gives them particular obligations and rights. This value system may explain also the relations between government and employers in training in Germany and Japan which so many British commentators would wish to replicate. They may not have noticed that the certificates of student attainment, bearing the imprimatur of the state, have a status which would make the rejection of their holders by employers or higher education institutions almost akin to treason.

Corporatism may be foreign to the USA which may have encouraged politicians and HMIs to look at American examples. Equally the community ideal—which propels the business involvement in American schooling—is alien to British conditions whatever the wishful thinking of ministers, for instance, in introducing City Technology Colleges. Perhaps they should have read the Friedman's complaint that American education was 'an island of socialism in a free-market sea' (Friedman M.and R., 1980).

The last area—of *social motivation*—less easily allows national categorization despite attempts to develop typologies of the collectivist/ individualist kind (McClelland, 1987). It is crucial, as HMIs noted, in Japan where the actual structure and organization of education seems of minor importance compared with the enormous commitment of all the participants to educational improvement. Social motivation is perhaps the least historically stable of all the types when applied at national level. Over a period of twenty or thirty years there has been a collapse of the great motivating ideals in large sectors of American society. The motivation of parents—and its links to values about power and participation clearly is still of major importance in assessing the relative achievements of British education compared with Germany or even France. Engendering popular motivation, if it is possible, is political rather than educational task of which the 1988 Education Reform Act is an example. This latter strategy in Britain is very different from the historical roots of educational motivation in most other industrial countries. Yet awareness of the differences is important when comparisons are made of educational achievements in other countries.

The kind of analysis suggested above is probably an anathema to the politicians and their conception of comparative education studies. It points out difficulties rather than identifying off-the-peg solutions. It gives emphasis to broader ideological issues. Yet such distaste of politicians should be regarded with suspicion. For educational policy in Britain since the mid-1980s has borrowed from other countries yet has transformed the foreign practices to fit in with particular British values. Parental representation in educational decision making has been increased through a succession of Education Acts to match levels of participation which had developed earlier than in other countries. Yet the corporatist and community values of elsewhere have been discarded in favour of a 'market' relationship between parents and schools. A national curriculum and regular assessment of students has been introduced to mirror continental European practice. In the process, the European model of elaborated aims and content which teachers have been trusted to implement and assess, has been turned on its head so that standardized assessment determines a curriculum almost without aims and with minimal content.

The politicians have borrowed then modified educational transplants to a British political environment. They have not had the same concern for authentic British traditions of teaching and learning as opposed to political concerns about consumer choice. It is in this area that educationists need to make their own comparative assessments. It is through empathetic appreciation of educational values elsewhere that distinctive British reforms may be developed.

What can be done with educational comparisons?

Is it possible to innovate successfully by copying foreign educational practice? If it is not, then what is the point of comparison? How can borrowing be fitted into authentic educational aims and practices? How can this selective borrowing be carried out?

Perhaps it is now impossible perfectly to reconcile comparison and authenticity and a more realistic instrumentality is the only viable course. So an abstract, external and ultimately alienating rationality may dominate teaching despite its failure to satisfy drives for individual identity or gestalt approaches to understanding because the world is driven by imperfect, instrumental and authoritarian rationality as many continental European writers have described (for instance Habermas,

1984). The achievement of authentic approaches to education may have to be confined to private relationships and experience as Rousseau recognized.

This dualism has been the basis of successful foreign educational borrowing in some instances. Japan's educational revolution after 1868 took alien educational forms from Europe, especially Germany (to which American forms were added less voluntarily during the occupation after 1945). These imports were designed to develop international economic competitiveness yet were never seen as anything else than alien forms with no real Japanese meaning. Authenticity was maintained by retaining Japanese approaches to moral education and a Japanese motivation towards a foreign educational content. Japanese analysis in the early twentieth century focused on means of reconciling Japanese values with western science especially through ideas such as moralogy (Hiroke, 1966).

Similarly, the import of the German research university into the USA from the end of the 19th century was in conflict with the American ideal of an egalitarian, homespun communalism. Yet traditional American educational values could not furnish the means to develop the knowledge base of the leading world economy that developed in the 20th century. The problem then became to reconcile the import with the local culture which has been a feature of the great debate about American education since the late 1950s and which has not been satisfactorily resolved.

There can be as many dangers in the successful reconciliation of imports and native traditions as in their compartmentalization. In Britain, foreign 'progressive' ideas of Friedrich Froebel and Maria Montessori through to Dewey were absorbed into an older, conservative, anti-egalitarian English individualism associated with John Locke. This may throw light upon the strange history of progressivism in the later twentieth century in Britain where it can be identified, by the 'right,' as alien radicalism and, a little earlier, by the 'left' as means of denying the cultural authenticity of working class children (Bernstein and Davies, 1969). Its particularity stands out when placed in a European setting. Celestin Freinet has been the most influential progressive educationist in France; Rudolf Steiner has dominated 'alternative' schooling in Germany; Ovide Decroly has a major influence Belgian education just as H.F.S. Grundtvig has on that of Denmark. Yet each of these progressives has had only the most marginal influence in Britain.

Comparison as a means to reinforce authenticity seeks justification in Rudyard Kipling's aphorism ('what should they know of England who only England know?'). Yet the spatial and cross-cultural perspective may have to be secondary to historical comparison. This is particularly important when politicians have implied, in making unfavourable comparisons between British and foreign education, that British weaknesses are the product of the educational history of the last thirty years. The contextual elements of international educational differences presented above should be explored historically in England more fully and critically. The weakness of the social egalitarian tradition in education in England compared with other countries in Europe and North America has been traced to the conquest of the dynamic forces of industrialism by a pre-industrial social structure in the nineteenth century (Weiner, 1985, Matthieson and Bernbaum, 1988). The failure to develop a corporatist state to lead social reform has been explored in the nature of English liberalism in the nineteenth century.

Other English educational weaknesses, revealed in contemporary cross-cultural comparison, need further historical analysis. If English traditions have excluded the emphasis on rationality, which is now to the benefit to continental European schools and societies, when and how did this happen in a country which has always been part of European intellectual culture? Perhaps the real villains included Thomas Arnold who attempted to emasculate British social and economic dynamism in the nineteenth century by turning its leaders into country gentlemen and whose pernicious influence has permeated every form of secondary school since then. Perhaps the list should include Locke who drew the rational revolutionary sting from the radical English Enlightenment of the seventeenth century to such an extent that the democratic, egalitarian alternative presented by Comenius to England in 1640 has been almost erased from folk memory. Or perhaps it was the cynicism of the early 18th century English establishment which started a process of preferring to allow Scots, from David Hume and Adam Smith to James Maxwell, to do the cool systematic thinking which the English disliked.

The answers to this wide ranging speculation cannot be predicted. They may produce surprising results if space is allowed for its investigation. This is comparison as enrichment. The challenge to the new realists is whether they are prepared to allow their encouragement for lateral thinking to take in deeper and wider perspectives and whether they can accept the conclusions that emerge. It is also a challenge to educationists to accept the value of achievements in other countries and to probe British educational traditions to find endogenous equivalents. Others, in areas ranging from industrial design to professional football, have faced similar challenges. Educationists should be able to match their responses.

What do these conclusions have for other kinds of comparisons—of pupils, teachers, schools, localities at particular moments of time? These activities may of course have different parameters but perhaps the same broad kind of judgement would apply. There may be national standards of achievement against which all must be judged for economic and social reasons which are similar to those that require international educational comparisons. Yet domestic comparisons may be used in the same way to give a spurious certainty to aspects of education which are much more complex. The same tensions between comparison and authenticity may operate. Comparisons between the attainments of students simply raise questions about the nature of personal development and of worthwhile understanding, appreciation and skill. Comparisons between teachers mean little without deeper understanding of the nature of teaching and of the teacher's place in the culture. Comparisons between schools and localities have to be placed in the context of concepts of community. This does not mean that comparison itself is illegitimate but that its ultimate purpose should be to stimulate local and authentic changes, which at the same time offers a different, though no less valuable, route from that followed by competitors.

REFERENCES

Archer, Margaret S (1979) *Social Origin of Educational Systems* London: Sage

Arnold, Matthew (1964) *Schools and Universities on the Continent* ed. Super R.H., Ann Arbor: University of Michigan Press

Beattie, Nicholas (1985) *Professional Parents: parent participation in four western European countries* Brighton: Falmer

Bernstein, Basil and Davies, Brian (1969) Some Sociological Comments on Plowden *Perspectives on Plowden* (ed.) Peters, Richard London: Routledge and Kegan Paul

Board of Education/Education Department (1897-1914) *Special Reports on Educational Subjects* 28 volumes London: HMSO

Bourdieu, Pierre and Gros, Francois (1989) Principes pour une reflexion sur les contenus d'enseignement *Le Monde de l'Education* April pp 15-18

Brereton, Cloudsley (1911) A Comparison between French and English Secondary Schools *Special Reports on Educational Subjects* Board of Education Vol 24 London: HMSO

Broadfoot, Patricia and Osborn, Marilyn French (1992) Lessons: comparative perspectives on what it means to be a teacher *Oxford Studies in Comparative Education* (ed.) Philips, David Vol 1 Wallingford: Triangle

Bronfenbrenner, Urie (1970) *Two Worlds of Childhood: US and USSR* London: George Allen and Unwin

Comenius, John Amos (1907) *The Great Didactic* London: Adam and Charles Black

Department of Education and Science (DES) (1967) *Children and their Primary Schools* Vol 1 London: HMSO

DES (1986) Press Release 1/86 London: DES

DES (1987a) Press Release 11/87 London: DES

DES (1987b) *Statistical Bulletin* 4/87 London: DES

DES (1988) Press Release 111/88 London: DES

DES (1989a) Press Release 6/89 London: DES

DES (1989b) Press Release 363/89 London: DES

DES (1990) Press Release 348/90 London: DES

DES (1991a) Press Release 2/91 London: DES

DES (1991b) Press Release 412/91 London: DES

DES (1992) Press Release 2/92 London DES

DES/ HMI (1986) *Education in the Federal Republic of Germany: aspects of curriculum and assessment* London: HMSO

DES/HMI (1987) *Aspects of Primary Education in The Netherlands* London: HMSO

DES/HMI (1989a) *The Provisional Teacher Program in New Jersey* London: HMSO

DES/HMI (1989b) *Aspects of Higher Education in the United States of America* London: HMSO

DES/HMI (1989c) *Initial Teacher Training in France: the training of secondary school teachers in the Academie de Toulouse* London: HMSO

DES/HMI (1989d) *Education in Denmark: aspects of the work of the folkeskole* London: HMSO

DES/HMI (1990a) *Aspects of education in the USA: teaching and learning in New York City schools* London: HMSO

DES/HMI (1990b) *Aspects of education in the USA: vocational and continuing education* London: HMSO

DES/HMI (1990c) *Core skills in further education* London: HMSO

DES/HMI (1991a) *Aspects of education in the USA: quality and its assurance in higher education* London: HMSO

DES/HMI (1991b) *Aspects of Vocational Education and Training in the Federal Republic of Germany* London: HMSO

DES/HMI (1991c) *Aspects of education in the USA: indicators in educational monitoring* London; HMSO

DES/HMI (1991d) *Aspects of Upper Secondary and Higher Education in Japan* London: HMSO
DES/HMI (1991e) *Aspects of Primary Education in France* London: HMSO
Dore, Ronald P. (1984) *Education in Tokuguwa Japan* London: Athlone
Dore, Ronald P. and Sako, Mari (1989) *How the Japanese learn to work* London: Routledge
Durkheim, Emile (1938) *The Rules of Sociological Method* (ed.) Catlin G.E.G. New York: The Free Press
Foxman, Derek (1992) *Learning Mathematics and Science* Slough: NFER
Friedman, Milton and Rose (1980) *Free to Choose* London: Secker and Warbourg
Fuhr, Christoph (1989) *Schools and Institutions of Higher Education in the Federal Republic of Germany* Bonn: Inter Nationes
Goodman, Roger (1990) *Japan's 'International Youth'* Oxford: Clarendon
Grant, Nigel (1979) *Soviet Education* 4th ed Harmondsworth: Penguin
Green, Andy (1990) *Education and State Formation* London: Macmillan
Habermas, Jurgen (1984) *Theory of Communicative Action* Vol 1 *Reason and the Rationalization of Society* London: Heinemann
Halls, W.D. (1976) *Education, Culture and Politics in Modern France* Oxford: Pergamon
Hans, Nicholas (1958) *Comparative Education* London: Routledge and Kegan Paul
Hearnden, Arthur (1976) *Education, Culture and Politics in West Germany* Oxford: Pergamon
Hiroke, Chikuro (1966) *The Characteristics of Moralogy and Supreme Morality* Kashiwa-Shi (Japan); Institute of Moralogy
Holmes, Brian (1981) *Comparative Education: some considerations of method* London: George Allen and Unwin
Holmes, Brian and McLean Martin (1989) *The Curriculum: a comparative perspective* London: Unwin Hyman
Hopper, Earl (1971) A Typology for the Classification of Education Systems *Readings in the Theory of Educational Systems* (ed.) Hopper, Earl London: Hutchinson
Husen, Torsten (ed) (1967) *International Study of Achievement in Mathematics* 2 vols. New York: John Wiley
Husen, Torsten (1987) Policy Impact of the IEA Research *Comparative Education Review* Vol 31 No 2 pp 29-46
Inkeles, Alex (1979) National Differences in Scholastic Performance *Comparative Education Review* Vol 23 No 3 pp 386-407
Jenkins, David (1980) Man: a course of study *Curriculum research and development in action* (ed.) Stenhouse, Lawrence London: Heinemann
Kant, Immanuel (1899) *Kant on Education* London: Kegan Paul, Trench and Trubner
Keep, Ewart (1991) The Grass Looked Greener-some thoughts on the influence of comparative vocational training research on the UK policy debate *International Comparisons of Vocational Education and Training for Intermediate Skills* (ed.) Ryan, Paul London: the Falmer Press

King, Edmund J. (1973) *Other Schools and Ours* 4th ed London: Holt, Rinehart and Winston

Kliebard, Herbert M. (1987) *The Struggle for the American Curriculum 1893-1958* New York: Routledge and Kegan Paul

Lapointe, A.E., Mead, N.A. and Philips, G.W. (1989) *A World of Differences* Princeton N.J.: Educational Testing Services

Lauglo, Jon (1983) Concepts of 'General Education' and 'Vocational Education' curricula for post-compulsory schooling in western industrialised countries *Comparative Education* Vol 19 No 3 pp 233-55

Lauwerys; Joseph A. (1965) Opening Address *General Education in a Changing World* Berlin; Max Planck Institute

Lawton, Denis and Gordon, Peter (1987) *HMI* London: Routledge and Kegan Paul

McClelland, David C. (1987) *Human Motivation* Cambridge: Cambridge University Press

McLean, Martin (1988) The Conservative Education Policy in Comparative Perspective *British Journal of Educational Studies* Vol 36 No 3 pp 200-217

McLean, Martin (1990) *Britain and a Single Market Europe: prospects for a common school curriculum* London Kogan Page/ Institute of Education

McNair, John M. (1984) *Education for a Changing Spain* Manchester: Manchester University Press

Maeroff, Gene I. (1991) *Teaching and Learning in English Urban Schools* Washington DC: Council of Great City Schools

Mallinson, Vernon (1975) *An Introduction to Comparative Education* 4th ed London: Heinemann

Marsh, Robert M. (1967) *Comparative Sociology* New York: Harcourt, Brace & World

Mathieson, Margaret and Bernbaum, Gerald (1988) The British Disease: a British tradition *British Journal of Educational Studies* Vol 28 No 2 pp 126-174

Mortimore, Peter *et al.* (1988) *School Matters* Wells: Open Books

National Commission on Excellence in Education (1984) *A Nation at Risk* Cambridge (Mass.): USA Research

National Economic Development Office/ Manpower Services Commission (NEDO/ MSC) (1984) *Competence and Competition: training and education in the Federal Republic of Germany, the United States and Japan* London:NEDO

Neave, Guy (1988) On the cultivation of quality, efficiency and enterprise: an overview of recent trends in higher education in Western Europe *European Journal of Education* Vol 23 No 1 & 2 pp 7-24

Noah, Harold J. (1987) Reflections *Comparative Education Review* Vol 31 No 1 pp 137-149

Noah, Harold J. and Eckstein, Max (1969) *Towards a Science of Comparative Education* London: Macmillan

Nuttal, Desmond L., Goldstein, Harvey, Prosser, Robert and Rasbach, John (1989) School Effectiveness *International Journal of Educational Research* 13 pp769-776

Organisation of Economic Cooperation and Development (OECD) (1974-) *Educational Statistics Yearbook* Paris: OECD

OECD (1990) *Education in OECD Countries 1987-1988: a compendium of statistical information* Paris OECD

OECD (1991) *Reviews of National Policies for Education: Netherlands* Paris: OECD

Prais, S.J. (1981) Some practical aspects of human capital investment: training standards in five occupations in Britain and Germany *National Institute Economic Review* No.98 pp.47-59

Prais, S.J. and Wagner, Karin (1985) Schooling Standards in England and Germany: some summary comparisons bearing on economic performance *National Institute Economic Review* No 112 pp. 53-76

Prais, S.J. (1986) Educating for Productivity: comparisons of Japanese and English. schooling and vocational preparation *Compare* Vol 16 No 2 pp 121-147

Prais S.J. and Wagner Karin (1988) Productivity and management: the training of foremen in Britain and Germany *National Institute Economic Review* No.123 pp. 34-45

Prais, S.J. and Beadle Elaine (1991) *Prevocational schooling in Europe today* Report Series No 1 London: National Institute of Economic and Social Research

Prost, Antoine (1990) Schooling and Stratification: paradoxes of the reform of the middle school in 20th century France *The Comprehensive School Experiment Revisited* (eds) Leschinsky, Achim and Mayer, Karl Ulrich Frankfurt am Main: Peter Lang

Purves, Alan C. (1987) The Evolution of the IEA: a memoir *Comparative Education Review* Vol 31 No 1 pp 10-28

Robitaille, D.F. and Garden, R.A. (1989) *The IEA Study of Mathematics II: contexts and outcomes of school mathematics* Oxford Pergamon

Rousseau, Jean Jacques (1911) *Emile* London: Dent

Ryan, Paul (ed.) (1991) *International Comparisons of Vocatonal Education and Training for Intermediate Skills* London: The Falmer Press

Sadler, Michael E. (1898) Problems in Prussian Secondary Schools for Boys *Special Reports on Educational Subjects* Education Department Vol 3 London: HMSO

Simons, Diane (1966) *Georg Kerschensteiner* London: Methuen

Steedman, Hilary (1987) Vocational training in France and Britain: office work *National Institute Economic Revuiew* No 120 pp. 58-70

Steedman, Hilary and Wagner, Karin (1989) Productivity, machinery and skills: clothing manufacture in Britain and Germany *National Institute Economic Review* No 128 pp. 40-57

Theissen, Gary L., Achola, Paul P.W. and Boakari, Francis Musa (1983) The Underachievement of Cross-National Studies of Achievement *Comparative Education Review* Vol 27 No 1 pp 46-68

Turner, Ralf H. (1971) Sponsored and Contest Mobility and the School System *Readings in the Theory of Educational Systems* (ed.) Hopper, Earl London: Hutchinson

UNESCO (1963-1991) *Statistical Yearbook* Paris: UNESCO
Walker, Rob and Adelman, Clem (1975) A *Guide to Classroom Observation* London: Methuen
Weiner, Martin J. (1985) *English Culture and the Decline of the Industrial Spirit 1850-1980* Harmondsworth: Penguin
White, Merry (1987) The *Japanese Educational Challenge* New York: Free Press

APPENDIX—INTERNATIONAL LEAGUE TABLES OF EDUCATIONAL PERFORMANCE

1. Student achievement

IEA mean scores (percentage correct responses) in mathematics of students aged 13-14

Country	1964	1982
Japan	44	62
Netherlands	34	58
France	26	54
Belgium	40	53
UK	27	49
USA	23	46
Sweden	23	43
Germany	n.a.	

Sources: Husen, 1967 Vol 2 pp.22
Robitaille and Garden, 1989 pp.105-119

2. Participation in education 1987-1988

Country	3 year olds	*Country*	4 years olds
France	96	France	100
Belgium	94	Belgium	98
(W) Germany	32	Netherlands	98
USA	29	(W) Germany	72
UK	26	UK	69
Japan	16	Japan	55
Netherlands	na	USA	49
Sweden	n.a.		

Country	17year olds in full-time education	*Country*	17year olds in full-time and part-time education
USA	89	Belgium	93
Japan	88	Japan	89
Belgium	88	USA	89
Sweden	83	Sweden	83
(W) Germany	82	(W) Germany	82
Netherlands	79	France	79
France	69	Netherlands	78
UK	34	UK	52

Percentages of 20 year olds in higher education (full-time and part-time)

Country	
Belgium	48
USA	36
Netherlands	32
France	31
UK	24
Sweden	9
Japan	na

Percentages of the relevant age group gaining second cycle (e.g. bachelor) higher education qualifications

Country	
USA	24
Japan	22
France	16
Belgium	15
UK	15
(W) Germany	13
Netherlands	8
Sweden	n.a.

3 Resources provided for education 1987-1988

Percentage of GNP devoted to public expenditure on education

Country	
Sweden	7.2
Netherlands	7.0
France	5.6
Belgium	5.1
Japan	5.0
UK	5.0
USA	4.8
(W) Germany	4.2

OECD *Education in OECD Countries 1987-1988: a compendium of statistical information* Paris OECD, 1990 p.107-109, 112-113, 115